Everything Shapes Itself to the Sea

poems by

James Plath

Finishing Line Press
Georgetown, Kentucky

Everything Shapes Itself to the Sea

For Zarina, and in memory of our friend Joseph Lynch

ACKNOWLEDGMENTS

With gratitude to Curwen Best and Joanne Diaz for their support,
and to the editors of journals and volumes in which
some of these poems first appeared:

The Caribbean Writer ("The Colonizers Return," "Sweet fuh Days")
Gulfstream Magazine ("Rumshop Woman")
Imported Breads: Literature of Cultural Exchange ("Islands")
National Forum ("A Priori")
Panhandler: a journal of poetry and prose ("Ringbang Theory")
The Poetry Porch ("Braveheart")
Rhino ("The Artist Wades for Inspiration")
Sunshine Magazine, Sunday Sun ("Out to Sea")
White Pelican Review ("Birdwatching, 8 a.m.")

"Ringbang Theory" and "The Colonizers Return" were reprinted in *Imported
Breads: Literature of Cultural Change* (2003)

Publisher: Leah Maines

Editor: Christen Kincaid

Cover Art: James Plath

Author Photo: Zarina Plath

Cover Design: Elizabeth Maines McCleavy

Printed in the USA on acid-free paper.
Order online: www.finishinglinepress.com
also available on amazon.com

Author inquiries and mail orders:
Finishing Line Press
P. O. Box 1626
Georgetown, Kentucky 40324
U. S. A.

Table of Contents

A Priori

"Repetition and recollection
are the same movement,
only in opposite directions."
Sören Kierkegaard

Yet, not all patterns push both ways.
The ribcage on a scallop shell expands
beyond breath, like branches mapping
unsettled sky, like hands raised at a calypso
tent, fingers pulled by the steady swell
of bass as it crests toward midnight,
moonlight, toward minute selves crammed
like powder into fireworks and launched
right through the stitched fabric of day.
So often, things around us want to be more:
footsteps on the garden path, thin columns
of newsprint, a passing thought, three
notes of a mini-bus horn that *decrescéndo*
around sharp corners, or breath enough
to extinguish a candle. There is no match
for a child's no, no power to counter
the infinite expansion that coils inside
even the tiniest package. So little
can some things be restrained or contained
that somewhere down this delicate line
all anyone can do is hold however fragile
a shell against an ear, and listen.

Ringbang Theory

So what if the days stretch
across this tin-roof horizon
like so many dominoes?

In Barbados, even silence
expands into octaves, casual
as roosters that amble past

rumshops—necks and
legs in precise movement,
cockscombs blaring in measures

of sun—unfazed by the fast breath
of buses, or the Rastafarians
that cycle past, singing for rain.

Seasons set the rhythm here
(tourists and hurricanes) and no one
needs to practice their scales. On the way

to Bridgetown, we pick up strains
of ringbang soca escaping from
chattel house windows as we hike,

like field hands, along a winding
hedgerow of limestone sidewalk,
trusting in drivers erratic as swallows.

Here cutlasses chime against stones
and swing against crops of weeds
that wedge between downpours; men

here labor in the intimacy of heat,
breaking to lie under a sprawl
of shade and fancy themselves

already done, already paid.
At Mall 34, we hold t-shirts
at arm's length, whirl, picture

loved-ones wearing them and
wait for change from a clerk
who sways, sings softly, as if

unaware she is anywhere anyone
would care what she did.
When there are only two

seasons, only two speeds, buses
are crowded and the air filters
laughter through the labyrinth

of coral that buoys us all up.
Hear those bones vibrate?
How can anyone ask for more?

Birdwatching, 8 a.m.
for Zarina

When I breathe the way one raindrop smells before
the sky unzips itself, when the nut of morning cracks open
and trills pour in through the open louvers, each note
a kingbird's plaintive cry, begging her mate to take off
and swoop in cat-stretch arc, to snatch food from mid-air
and tuck it into her grateful throat, red as last night's sunset;

When I witness doves dancing on the patio through the vapors
of our morning coffee, heads curling like tender vines, or recall
the easy passion of calypso that drifts from the port at night and
laps against the shores of our sleep, I begin to think all I really need
is to be with you, maybe help each other pry open this geode
world with the loving precision of a kingbird's beak.

The Angle of Opalescence

In buoyant shallows on the deep side
of froth, I arch my back, floating and trying
to coax my wife to go beyond the breakers,
past the broken shells and burgoo roil.

Anything that floats is spared the bump
and grind, the rhythmic tumbling that
turns jagged pieces of glass, over time,
into opaque and opalescent charms.

With a coating of sea salt, her milk-glass
skin glitters like a prima ballerina
in muted light, so that when her arms
and legs catch the cusp of foam and

she rolls, mesmerizingly, up and down
the rough slope of gravel, this curtate
sonata plays itself out so quickly that,
from my angle, everything looks beautiful.

Island

"When he left the beach the sea was still going on."
Derek Walcott (Omeros LXIV: III)

When it's cloudy, the water begins
to look like aged rum, and the same birds
circling promise that whatever powerful
weed can't be smoked or hacked down
today can occupy vast tomorrows.

Anything is possible when the sea pulls
tankers and cruise ships from thin air,
the churn of propellers and the swell of
their horns sending wakes, false tides,
against seawall and beach. Winds cup

the sails of catamarans that skip waving
tourists along the leeward coast, while
the pirate-themed party boat slips past
daylight, past dusk, its "crew" flashing
bright as cooked lobsters, or the pale

sides of flying fish. Everything shapes
itself to the sea. To the sprat fishermen
working their gill nets with the relaxed
concentration of surgeons, every breast
and bare butt must look the same.

Ebb Tide

The sea rides high on the horizon
today, spreading itself like applause
over silence, like candlewax over
watermarked paper, sealing the island
unofficially off. At ebb tide, beach boys

transparent as sand crabs sidestep
their way onto blankets and towels,
fingers kneading muscles or spots
needing lotion quicker than anyone can
slip a bookmark or beg for pardon.

Ever "have a black mahn?" or seen
a "big bamboo" in action? They're
part of the package: a touch, a few
memories—minimum wage, a few
dollars or, better, a place to sleep.

On the jetty where a fisherman casts
his net into glare, waves wash over the
rocks that make him look tall, Christlike,
lapping at the edges of day. Children
splash each other and circle, sing

as they gather sea-glass rendered
magically round to skip into blue infinity,
bending low as they throw so the pieces
seem to skim right into the carnival
mouth of the sun as it tries to duck.

When the sea retreats, even tourists
grow bold. Vacation mentality depends
on such things, such sleight of hand.
Only nurse sharks lolling on the bottom,
oblivious to the reef fish that nose around

coral, can send them crawling back
to shore in an easy panic, breathless,
full of exhilaration that will grow,
quickly, into exaggeration. Hear the
music build, the string section tighten?

When the sea recedes, the self expands.
After all, who will know? It's money
well spent. At ebb tide, all things seem
possible with the right music, and no one
takes anything too seriously.

Jetsam

for Zarina

Even in flannel, wearing sleep

in your hair, now, like hibiscus
tucked carelessly behind one ear,

the sight of you rubbing dreams
from your eyes is enough to pull me
toward you with the certainty of tides,

savoring again the smell of your skin
in seawater, buoyed by our laughter
and the strength the salt gave you
to carry me over a threshold of coral

—or the sight of you wearing sea-
green silk under a canopy of lights
strung like pearls at a cliffside
restaurant, when velvety mantas glided
past in thigh-high water and you

wondered how they'd feel wrapped
around our legs—or the way, later,
in the lace-patterned light that filtered
through our window, we moved along
each other's lines of contour and motion,
ever grateful for our abandon.

Double Jeopardy at Door #3
for the men at Paradise Hideaway rumshop

Colin says that windows and doorways
shape the world, "Like a television set,
wouldn't you say so, Mister Lynch?"
The analogy pulls him into a medley
of American game shows he loves
to watch on the island's only channel.
Mister Lynch towels off one of six
glasses behind the bar and nods, though
the former Barbados policeman is certain
regimen gives the world shape, and he
says so after slamming down the glass:
"Discipline! *Dat is de main ting!*"

And Leroy? The only other customer
eyes me carefully, his gold tooth glinting.
Silence shapes Leroy's world, and it's
clear he's uncomfortable saying what's true
for anyone else. The proprietor, all nervous
energy, is arranging cardboard coasters
on the counter to illustrate his point. On
Black Rock Road, buses choke off
the beginnings and ends of every sentence.
Middles are taken by children in uniforms
who, passing, recite their "Good Evenings"
as they file into undisciplined dusk.

When I hear my own name and realize
they want me to settle things right then
and there, I'm staring so long through
the open double-doorway at telephone lines
that crisscross so crazily over neighbors'
houses and breadfruit trees, sea haze
encroaching upon the horizon, everything
starts to look abstract as a TV test-pattern.
One more snap of rum and I begin to feel

my voice jump right onto those wires, half-
wired myself and trying so hard not to fall
that I can't help but fully entangle myself.

Rumshop Woman

"Home is where the art is."
West Indian journalist John Wickham

Seagulls flutter overhead, steamships,
sailboats aim for shore where she leans

on a table shaped like an African
djembe, her brown skin painted taut

as a drumhead, hair tressed out in
waves that beat against the shore of

every Bajan man's fantasy. Her nipples
are the size of cigarettes—cigarettes

the size of fingers, two butts smoldering
in the ashtray in front of her, her dress

the color of sun and sand. This woman
has lips that are purple as deep-water

patches before "weather" comes, purple
eye shadow more nervous water.

It would do no good to warn her that
the same young artist has spread her all over

St. Michael's parish wearing the same skimpy
dress the color of a wish-you-were-here

sunset. Nor would it do any good to take her
to see the walls of an Eagle Hall rumshop

where her dress is hiked up, legs wrapped around
an unzipped man. Whether that's all in her past or

her future, her face on this wall tells you nothing
matters anymore—that even you don't matter.

Her eyes look implacidly away from you,
you rumshop men who swivel on stools to gawk

at her, to remind yourselves what real women must
look like. Her creator made them cat-shaped,

black and mysterious as the sea at night. But
on the wall of this shop, under a soft lunar

fluorescence, they look as far away as
the eyes of a Banks Beer poster model

standing on a paper beach in a deep
horseshoe bikini bottom, ripped t-shirt

hanging over each breast like a fighter's
towel, hair tucked under a baseball cap.

With the rum model, writhing against
a backstage wall while a saxaphonist tries

to heat up onstage, ostensibly
poised to sing jazz between two

steel pans, her legs a scissor-shadow
in a white backlit evening gown, it's more

of the same: None of them ever look you in
the eye, as if looking would *change* things.

Outside, a tall slender Rasta man in blue
jeans, dreadlocks piled high on his head,

is followed by a short and stocky woman
hanging onto his pants as they walk

and talk. On this island, like so many
in the Caribbean, it's not easy to hold

onto anything, much less a man. As this
rumshop woman waits each day for barstools

to fill, her eyes say only that this outside
woman knows. Overhead, sea gulls circle

expectantly, scavenger birds hoping
to pick up the pieces that fall each day,

regular as tropical rains—a storm so frequent
that you begin to think it's natural.

On Suttle Street

Don' go dere, mahn,
our young driver says, as we bend
along Spring Garden Highway,
past youngsters splashing
at Brighton, the nearby refinery
puffing like a chain smoker.
Drugs, bad scene, why you ask?
Past young boys tackling a giant
street version of table tennis,
their paddles big and threatening.

Just curious,
we tell him, not wanting to admit
we just came from there, errant
explorers looking for the Indian
merchants' row but discovering
spice instead. On Suttle Street,
we drew people to doorways,
incredulous as we passed,
until we neared the end
of the street and three shirtless
men stepped out of the shadows
to block our advance, others closing
around us like humid air.

All right!
I said, smiling nonchalantly, and walked,
holding my wife's hand, between them,
through them, kept walking with her
though the air around us began
to feel like a bucket of water
overwarmed by a firebrand sun
plunged into sizzle. Two magic
words my rumshop friend taught me
the night before to prove I am
no cruise ship tourist—though
my hands will still tremble ever
so slightly over evening coffee,
as if the concrete patio was
listing, port to starboard.

Out to Sea

"The whole area is flooded;
about 14 houses have been washed away;
Carew is out to sea on a rooftop."
Roger Worrell
on the Voice of Barbados

Like James Dickey's stewardess,
        sucked from a fuselage into a spiral
of spent lives, the old calypsonian
        saw death coming from far away.

He saw it as the shoreline diminished,
        saw it in the unbelievable waves and
debris that tumbled into the swell: the stoves
        and fridges, bits of lumber, utility wires.

He saw it years before the strange lightning-
        less thunder sent a boulder rolling
in the run-off through Weston, saw it bearing
        down on him at the financial office

where he tried, unsuccessfully, to buy
        a house far away from the low-lying
fishing village, closer to the music of Bridgetown.
        He saw it in the faces of lawyers who told this

black man they could not help, and in the clouds
        that lingered over the island, each drop
of rain an accumulation—his own bitter cup
        to eventually drink. He saw, in every splash

of surf, an erosion he thought only he could
        perceive, an hourglass running out
on him—he who lived on an island
        and, like so many, could not swim. He

saw it in the dreams that saturated his
            sheets and swept his chattel house out
to sea, again and again, each time more real
            than the songs that gave him sustenance.

What he could not see were the thousands
            of black armbands worn at Kadooment
during Crop Over Festival, or the white
            pastor who would punish him for years

of faithful non-attendance by setting him up
            as a bad example: the man who built
his house on sand, the foolish man whose
            spiritual foundation was more uncertain

than the jigsaw of coral rock that bore up
            his and so many other island dwellings.
In earlier times, De Great Carew, so abruptly
            and dramatically taken away, might

have been compared to Elijah and his grand
            exit, speeding off on a meteor
everyone swore was a fiery chariot
            drawn by white horses, God's taxi.

But swept out to sea, last seen pleading
            to the birds for help, the old calypsonian
could only cling to his music, filling the air
            with myth, this starry night.

Panacea

With the moon still lingering
in the slow swirl of dawn,
our bedsheets moistened
by sleep, we hear a parade

of Bajans, plastic buckets in hand,
head-ties and boots, clattering
and laughing as they walk
past our window on their way

to the beach. Last night, after
Iris came calling, bending palms
in the courtyard until they looked
like catapults aiming coconuts

at constellations, we floated
like pearls in an old shampoo
commercial. Now, as I struggle
to position myself against dawn,

I see scavenger tools and wonder
what swept onto sand besides us?
The sea is a healer, one man
told us yesterday. Inside-out,

it would fix us "right up." Such
is vastness, able to diminish, able
to dilute. Such is salt, able to cure.
And things still left to discover.

Still Life, with Breadfruit

At the abandoned resort
a dog melts
into surf
that rises
like just another
dune of sand,
its paddling
suspended
as the gulls
that hang
overhead
or the guard
cast as shadow
from a West Indian
almond.
Three Germans
and a British
exchange student
turn every ten minutes
in the rotisserie
sun. A beach
boy who's tried
them days
before
stretches, eyes
closed, in a
thicket
of shade,
so that
when this
bounty
floats in,
there's no
one to race
us, no one
at all.

The Artist Wades for Inspiration

These things have a way
of working out, the tide
pulled back
at the slightest shrug
of lunar suggestion—
white-bellied waves
that curl short-
sheeted into the wind.

She thinks bland
retinal recognition
holds her back, that her
thoughts are not even fresh
as the dimpled moments
her toes leave for wet, shell-
less sand to consider.
Along the foam-line

She fancies a row of painters
painting, easels wrapped
like wooden peg-legs
in strands of gray-green
seaweed. Fingers of water tug
at their cuffs with child-
like impatience, and why
not? Hasn't she read that
the human body is seventy-
some percent water? Haven't
the fluid cycles of women
been joined, as if by
invisible cord, to a moon-
faced puppeteer? Pulled now,
by the waterline's slow retreat
toward a wispy horizon,

She spots an upturned fighting
conch, its fragile, calcified
spiralling tip left somehow
untouched by the swirling
of currents, suspended gravel.
And she tells herself that
erosion exposes new surfaces—
at least, the illusion of new
ground to cover. Overhead,
a swash of high-pitched
white sweeps suddenly past:
Don't look, she thinks, as she
takes the shell in hand and
flings it at a flock of seagulls
everyone has seen before.

The Colonizers Return

Even with warning—a glint of wing
or a ship's horn herald—their skin is

shockingly pink, the folds of
affluence more pronounced.

And they hide, always: wallets
in camera bags, cameras in

fanny packs, credit cards in socks,
and eyes behind glasses gradually tinted

like the windows in stretch limousines.
But it's obvious most are new to this,

assuming the (im)position for one or two
weeks and hoping to avoid discovery

as much as discomfort or danger.
Tonight, a full moon hazed by clouds

pulls at the sea, at the percent of each
that owes obeisance, pulls calls from

the island roosters who fall each time
for this age-old trick, the way whistling

frogs take up their cause on days when
the sun is shut down for a spell. But

none of them, wearing those sad-eyed no-
blink Buckingham faces, ever seems to notice.

They do everything in a determined way,
whether bathing in storm clouds or hiking

in mist: they've saved for this trip,
you know, put off repairs on the Volvo

or house, even fallen behind on a utility
or two—but they'd die before they'd

let you know, preferring instead a
protracted death, a monthly death at

eighteen percent. You can tell by the
way they hold the pen each time with

the careful concentration of a schoolchild
learning her cursive, trying to keep the

pen from betraying them as they sign here,
sign there, sign to each other—as if no one

were watching them argue in mime over
how much West Indian waitstaff are worth.

Sweet fuh Days

Dominoes shape the mornings
at Pearle's, arranged like a geometry
of side streets whose crossroads
always seem to meet here.

On a small wooden table topped
with corrugated, players slam
their cards with the force of light
that pries through the bars of this

rumshop's windows and the
force of every bad hand that
anyone here has ever been dealt.
But it's only play. Traffic on

Black Rock moves to high tide.
At sunrise, only hours ago,
cruise ships poured their cargoes
of cameras and sunglasses

onto the docks, a parade wobbling
down the gangplank like the doves
here that amble toward crumbs,
getting their bearings, their land legs,

their go here, turn here, wait
here customer's-always-right
voice. Later, when everyone's
had their fill, some of the taxi

drivers will come to this place
for a snap of rum or a cold Banks
beer to watch the players still
slamming them down and chattering:

Ah tell ya, boy, me drink so much
and dance so much me ca hardly
remember she name, me was so
sweet, so sweet fuh days!

The drivers will laugh and shake
their heads, maybe set a fresh bottle
of white rum on the table—their own
cargoes of stories bursting at the hold.

Proper Chicken

No one hides in Paradise
Hideaway for long—not even Joe,
who owns the place and a second
property on Government Hill
guarded by a pair of Great Danes.

Stretching like a dog after his nap,
Joe appears from the back room
as a shirtless, shoeless man
tries to enter the rumshop and
Joe cocks an air backhand that

staggers the man, sends him back
to the sidewalk. *Proper chicken,*
he cries, *for your dogs, Mr. Lynch,*
and at Joe's wagging finger
he sets the five-gallon pail down

then names a price that drops
the instant Joe lifts the lid and the
smell knocks him back. *This chicken
is spoiled. I don't want it.* But he
does, and he gets it all for three

flying fish—three Barbados
dollars—because of that look,
the same one I saw last week
at his gonnabe guest house before
we swung cutlasses shoulder

to shoulder to teach the impudent
weeds and tree-sprouts a lesson,
when Joe had to kick aside a stray
cat that had died right there
on his concrete steps, the two dogs

inside, oblivious. Wearing a headscarf
I swung my cutlass until my hands
became red-raw reluctant. After
the man leaves, Joe leaves, and I'm
left watching his rumshop because

I knew where he keeps the cold
Banks, how to pour a snap of rum,
and I understood the chicken
wouldn't last long in the tropical
heat if he didn't leave right away.

*And maybe I go into Bridgetown
to see de man about a permit,* Joe says.
At dusk Colin straddles his usual seat, eyes
me suspiciously. *Where's Mister Lynch?*
I tell him and Colin explodes

with laughter. *Ho boy, he be jokin'
you, jokin' you good!* In the bruise-
colored night men walking past call
All right? and Colin echoes, *All right?*
Yadokay, they chime and it startles

me to see a confused-looking Leroy
appear next to Colin, the gray stubble
on his face suddenly scratchy. *Well,*
Colin says, *I'm off to take a sea bath.*
For the next half-hour Leroy sits,

my only customer, not saying a word
except to order a second snap of
rum and another glass of tapwater.
I wash the glasses as I've seen Joe
do every day, towel and arrange them

neat as the smile I flash Leroy, feeling
like a "proper" bartender. *You know,*
Leroy finally says, *I never taut I'd live
to see de day when a white man serve
a black man on Black Rock Road.* I

start to tell him I never thought of it
like that, only one friend helping
another, but Leroy dismisses the idea
with a backhanded wave and says his
son is probably looking for him. Long

after he leaves I'm still bathed in the
fishbowl light of the rumshop, staring
into deep-sea darkness when I am
stiffened by a rumpus, a swish of
trousers, four inauspicious

shadows gliding past. *Hey White
Mahn!* one of them shouts as
the group slows to near-stop.
Down the road, in Paradise
Villas, my wife is worrying, doubtless

annoyed I missed dinner. *All right?*
I call, thinking of her and those big
dogs tearing into that spoiled chicken,
find myself sated when I hear the men
say, as they amble away, *Yadokay!*

Shell Games

Outside Broad Street stores, nestled like birds
against chimneys, old women cradle the cloth of their
skirts between knees hard and porous as coral, balancing

baskets divided neatly as their days: pigeon peas
to measure, gnarled pods to shell. Unlike merchants
down the street, they never bargain, seldom speak,
their hands working with a magician's quickness. Even
indifference to dreadlocks, to sunburnt shoppers

in Bermuda shorts, is meted out in equal measure.
As sunlight edges toward their hands and bodies
on the sidewalks thin, their fingers work even more

urgently, slick as dusk and quick as hoes, turning
peas and pods into a blur of sod-colored knuckles,
the way children roll marbles or rocks in their hands,
imagining them whole planets. It's the game
they play, and everyone has some version

of those old copper measures, peas cupped into
hands like drinks of cool water and poured
into pints. Later, behind some Bank

Hall curtains pretending to be glass,
pots of pigeon peas and rice will bubble,
imaginations adding meat.

Neptune's

We're in deep water
again, a snapper's length
from an elderly couple
with British accents—all
pinkies and whispers and
proper nouns: Paris, Cannes,
St. Maarten's, Grand Cayman.

In front of us, a convention
of spoons and knives and
forks—ten in all. Recessed
against mahogany walls,
saltwater fish tanks bubble
and the waiter, rigid
as a drink stirrer, offers
us three kinds of service:
slow, *lezzurely*, or fast.

There is no laughing in this
darkened wine cellar,
so we tickle each other
with sidelong glances,
knee-nudge banter,
nonetheless careful
to keep a close eye
on the Brits so that we can
grab the right fork when
comes our first
lezzurely course.

Braveheart

for Norman Plath

Today, while Antillean bullfinches stiffen
their wings and hop defiantly against each
other on our patio tiles, brave but comic
as Mel Gibson in a kilt, I think of you,

strong-jaw stubborn and battling five
days longer than any of your doctors
predicted—as if to make your joke come
true, to pay them back for all the hours

you waited for them in stiff-backed chairs
and grumbled to Mother, always too loudly,
What's the sense of having an appointment?
Hours after the call, I'm still dumbfounded

by these tiny birds, watching their nervous
movements and realizing how their own hearts
must beat quick as a hummingbird's, fluttering
fast as the rapid eye movement that wings us

into the land of dreams—a netherworld that pays
us back for the lives we've led when we're awake.
When we first came to this coral island, godlike
we took to naming birds, to try to reflect

the subtle quirks that set them apart, these
otherwise identical dusty-gray sparrows.
One bullfinch called "Spike" used his wings
for balance, like a fighting cock, spurs kicking

up a concrete fuss, while another we had to call
"Earful" because of the way she'd sputter and
scold like an athlete going nose-to-nose
with an umpire, shrieking, wings flapping

like chattering teeth from a novelty store.
But today I'm reminded of "Pegleg," one
we thought a con man, a pirate who came
to us first every morning, as if the others

had sent him to turn us to dough, to prompt
our return with bread to crumb. He'd pose
like a beggar on our patio rail sans tin cup,
one leg retracted like an airplane wheel,

balancing without the slightest hint of wobble
or strain. Then we noticed the tumor at first
joint—watched it grow, as if our daily ration
had nourished it too. One day Pegleg flew off

and returned weeks later without a foot:
Doctors be damned, he had chewed himself
well, re-created himself to fit the nickname
we had bestowed, as if to acknowledge

that here in Barbados almost everyone
has another name, one they've earned
on the streets, in the schools, a name
that tells the whole story—secrets and all.

Everyone has a dead father poem, a hospital
poem, a tribute poem, and I know you'd be
the first to say you'd want none of this
sappiness or bluff and bluster. But watching

these birds that hop on countertops and fly through
louvered windows as they please, I can't help
but think of your own irreverence—like
the time we were fishing and you suddenly

stood to relieve yourself, rocking the boat
and grinning, "You know what they say:
If you can't *catch* them . . . ," then
leaving a ten year old's mind to finish.

Watching these birds and thinking of one
in particular who finally flew off, brave
as Earhart, into the past, I can't help but
remember your own resilience, your own

resourcefulness, the lesson you took
thirty years to explain: Anyone can
learn to stand on two feet; you
taught me to balance on one.

Margins

By the careenage, in the wake
of sunlight that separates
      mangos and paw-paws
            from golden apples and plums,
water slaps against concrete and a young woman
rises before us like a rake we've just stepped on,
handing us a coupon for an outrageous discount
at a playground hotel. All we have to do is
      blah-blah-blah,

but then somehow, something gives
us away and her lips pull taut as runner's sinew:
      How long you here?
When I say four months, she snatches it back.
      You almos' Bajan! Don' be pullin' nutin'
      on me now, Cousin, dis only for tourists,
      and me got three children to feed.

That night, sprawled on separate twin beds
the staff pushed together once they knew
we were married, we listen to
      tree frogs mist over dusk, suddenly
      gradual as the colors that blend
      in the Rastafarian market,
and consider, still,
      if we aren't tourists, what *are* we?

Then we plot like conspirators to storm
the island with one last fling before we fly
back into the eye of winter, wondering
      if we have enough money for
      black belly sheep and conch
            or need to eat eddoes and breadfruit
again, and whether we'll taxi or squeeze into
      the mini-buses we've taken by day,
      the only whites, wearing
      our three-star apparel.

James Plath is R. Forrest Colwell Chair and Professor of English at Illinois Wesleyan University, where he has taught since 1988. In a past life he edited the award-winning *Clockwatch Review: a journal of the arts* and directed the Hemingway Days Writers' Workshop & Conference in Key West. A published poet, fiction writer, and journalist, Plath was invited to lecture as a Fulbright Scholar at the University of the West Indies-Cave Hill Campus, in Barbados for a semester, and these poems grew out of that experience.

His poetry was previously collected in *Courbet, on the Rocks* (White Eagle Coffee Store Press, 1994) and included in *City of the Big Shoulders: An Anthology of Chicago Poetry* and *Men of Our Time: An Anthology of Male Poetry in Contemporary America*. Also the author-editor of six scholarly books on Ernest Hemingway, John Updike, Ray Carver, and the film *Casablanca*, Plath is the happily married father of six and grandfather of seven.